# MALFORMED CONFETTI

Juliet Cook

**MALFORMED CONFETTI**

Poems © 2018 by Juliet Cook
julietcook.weebly.com

Cover art *Angeline* ©2018 by Simona Candini
simonacandini.com

Crisis Chronicles #102
ISBN: 978-1-64092-973-9
1st edition, 1st printing, 125 copies

Published 16 October 2018 by
Crisis Chronicles Press
3431 George Avenue
Parma, Ohio 44134 USA

crisischronicles.com
ccpress.blogspot.com
facebook.com/crisischroniclespress

## Deadly Doll Head Dissection

Doll head fantasyland, fun-filled dollies, licking dollies, slurping dollies, yummy dollies, gummy dollies, genuflecting dollies, dick sucking dollies, doll gags, doll debauchery, a sipping, slipping, discombobulated dolly.

A doll thought she was being drunk sweetly. A doll thought she was softly peeking, but she was peaking like an anorexic doll head turning black. Like a servile ugly duckling with a deviated septum soon to be a cunt doll, an asshole doll, a stinky dolly douche bag, a bitchy doll injection mold disaster. Bleeding doll, broken doll, doll head rape. Shackled doll, spasmed doll, mangled doll, impaled doll, unglued doll legs, smashed doll brain.

Deadly doll head dissection. A dolly crematorium, an almost life less doll. A doll scatterbrained, a doll agitating until it barfs up more awful doll head gobbledygook. A spitting and hacking doll. Spinning, falling and flailing inside the doll vomitorium. A dark doll somnambulating and throwing up.

A doll hurling jerky truffles, a doll unfurling quirky squiggles. A scary doll giggles then explodes like a dollcano. A bloody shimmering doll. A hotly whirring doll. A rising up doll head. A transforming doll brain. A doll biting back until penile balloons hiss then deflate....

## 1. Beginnings — Hideously Edible Girlie Dolls

- Self Portrait as a Slab on a Slab ........... 3
- Scene ........... 4
- Necking ........... 5
- assembly line doll head roach hotel ........... 6
- Doll Head Obscenity ........... 7
- Balut ........... 8

## 2. Rank Middles — (Pseudo)Surgically Enhanced Female Creatures

- Self Portrait as Stuffed Pepper ........... 13
- Catwalk ........... 14
- Cleavage ........... 15
- Mass Production ........... 17
- Firecracker firecracker boom boom splatter paint ........... 18
- Say she had dirty follicles ........... 19
- Stubble ........... 20
- Meat Chorus ........... 21
- Threesome ........... 22
- Plague ........... 23
- Self-Lubricating ........... 24
- Deer Head Variations ........... 25
- Mutating Cosmetic Surgery ........... 27
- Ladyfingers ........... 29
- Domestic Disturbance ........... 30
- Snake in a Can Gag ........... 32
- Venus Tree ........... 33
- Saint Lucy Eyes ........... 34

## 3. Gradually Ebbing Down — (Para)Normal Uncertain Wives

- Semiabstract Self Portrait ........... 39
- Ghost Teeth ........... 40
- Parasitic Twin ........... 41

—The New Witchery.................................................................43
—The Ugly Duckling.................................................................44
—The Moth................................................................................45
—The Swan...............................................................................46
—The Sugar Glider...................................................................47
—Dead Raven............................................................................48
—The Pig Box............................................................................49
—A Song....................................................................................51
—Sieve......................................................................................52
—The Paper Dolls....................................................................53
—Haunted Sea Urchin.............................................................55
—Giant Squid...........................................................................56
—Hydra.....................................................................................57
—Another Medusa..................................................................58
—Volary....................................................................................59
—seamstress of the belly of the beast...............................60
—Purple Speculum.................................................................61
—Volatility...............................................................................62
—Coiled....................................................................................63

4. Suddenly Ebbing Further Down — (Ab)Normal Waves on the Brink

—dream about being..............................................................67
—Marmalade Glaze................................................................68
—Red Shrink Wrap..................................................................69
—Mauvette Maroon................................................................70
—Angioplasty Show................................................................71
—Crepuscular Creep...............................................................72
—Arterial Discombobulation................................................73
—Broken Blister Pearls..........................................................74
—The Fortune Teller...............................................................76
—Mortuary Cabinet................................................................77
—Love Can Be a Chokecherry...............................................78

viii

—Red Moon Ashes...... 79
—Red Lunatic...... 80
—Blue Marriage...... 81

## 5. Off & On Flow — Almost Drowning, But Then Resurging

—Why I Dye My Hair Red...... 85
—Sucker Punch...... 86
—Vintage Pom Pom Underwater...... 87
—Contorted Impregnation...... 88
—Drain Potion...... 89
—My sorrow is not something you can eat...... 90
—Insecticide Dye Job...... 91
—How Many Holes Can You Handle?...... 93
—Spew...... 94
—Spawning...... 95
—Viral Spiral...... 96
—Un-sided Self Portrait...... 97

—About the Author...... 99

—Acknowledgments & Notes...... 101

# 1. Beginnings — Hideously Edible Girlie Dolls

## Self Portrait as a Slab on a Slab

I'm a little slice of pound cake in a little coffin,
served with a little container of half & half.
Where will you pour the creamer?

I'm a cut off braid with silver threads,
served on a silver platter. Split ends
unloose themselves from multiple strands.

I'm a slab on a slab, a plait on a plate,
a poorly shorn lamb on the lam.
I'm sweet, heavy, deathly, hairy.
I'm shaved, heaving, dripping, dirty
with my ruffled bloomers torn off
at the stems. So throw me in. Fast forward

my declension. Will I thrash or gulp?
Will I sink or float? Will I suck it all up
like a sugary sea sponge with teeth?

**Scene**

It's hazy something like
lightning bugs without their lights.

If girls were flying insects,
then you could rip off their wings.
If girls were soft thoraxes,
then you could cut

out what makes them glow.

I crawl around hiding my wings.
I throb on & off underneath
a dark shell. Most of the time,
none of you can see me, but

every once in a while I'm a flare,
then I'm an accident scene

**Necking**

The cooties turn into ravenous parasites.
The girl germs desperately hurl
like tiny razorblade boomerangs.
Her fingers are fleshy ribbons wrapping themselves
around the necks of pet birds who must be hanged.

Pet kittens must be drowned in dirty janitor's mop water.
Pet poodles must be pummeled with stained lucky stones.
Her legs are pumice stoned and shaved, packaged
with dead electric eel and nobody's touching that appetizer,
so bristly in spite of ministrations. Her not so pretty ponies

are tethered in a circle. The rope is chafing.
The pony ride turns into a back-seat Tilt-O-Whirl
without room to maneuver away from smashed Milk Duds,
wet wads gobbed to sticky seat. Turkey neck pops in her head.
Gobble gobble. Mottled wattles. Dark meat. The wishbone snap.

### assembly line doll head roach hotel

doll wig hackling
pulling hairy erections out
tiny holes in rubber scalp
then snip, snip, snip

tiny holes in bisque scalp
require more attention
paid to the coiffure
the mind drifts again to courtesans,
hard candy crotch, overheated ceramics,
steamy mass in a basin, candied brain stem

dopamines cut off with dull silver
blade strokes, guillotined heads lobbed,
hairline fractures oozing
gel into the sale bin

the mind drifts again to cock
roaches laying eggs in the cracks
of hollow pates, baby doll bug gut
follicular fusion, planting a roach hotel
inside the head inserted via empty eye hole
then inserting the eye; now she's a death's head,

a corpse vat, a decorative vessel for rot,
a pretty little toddler faced creepy crawly
urn with perfect hairdo, with pink bow
lips, the gift behind which insecticide breeds

**Doll Head Obscenity**

This one is not a still-life, but it might as well be
because I'm trapped inside
this battered bisque pate; these googly eyes
tilted sideways. Stuck off-kilter.

Whirring around me like a machinated halo,
the constantly circling steel molds
mass produce another batch of prettier,
smoother, more seamless heads

and everyone buys them. Everyone wants
to lick them, kiss them, affix them
to the latest sexy bed springs.
The latest seductive mattress coverings.

The paint is flaking off my lips.
It looks like dried blood. It looks like shit.
Even my hissy fits are unglossy.
Even the doll hospital won't touch me

no matter how I plead for them to reset my eyes.
My voice is a wan green mushy pea squishing past
these gold-shellacked wish bones I'm choking on.
These chloroform-soaked apricot cookies

with their dainty scalloped edges
and poison-saturated centers.
They have numbed my tongue.
They have fractured my cranium.

They have brainwashed me into obsolescence.

## Balut

1.
The albino children file in, boy/girl
except upon closer inspection all of them
red-eyed girls.

Saucy noodle dishes flung inside
Tilt-O-Whirls until the sauce dripped off;
got sucked into a vortex.

All the jewelry to fill their holes
swirling in the autoclave.

2.
Once upon a time I wished to be wan
with black tips. Sooty tern in place of heart,
pecking, pecking. The shell cracks; it seeps
bone meal. Furry poltergeists sip from

my marrow like maggots
working a wound, little sinners
to digest the dead flesh until
the fur bristles.

It looked like a suckling pig between the legs
again, but one of my holes was birthing
a whole peccary.

3.
Duck duck goose swine, plumped up
with peccadilloes. I paid for these holes,
so I wear the jewelry.

Extracted from a bucket of sand,
the bones that seem firm
will be tender when cooked,

when eaten while it is still warm
in its shell. White fragments, pink inside.

**Self Portrait as Stuffed Pepper**

Precocious green glowing outside, gutted inside.
Like an alien on a plate, posing as an edible self
portrait. I just might be designed for consumption.
I might be a messy quick fix, stowing secretly

a choking hazard in the midst of flapping lips.
Before you take off my flabbergasted flapper lid
and inspect for saucy or seedy trickery; see what I am
cooking in here, what I've been stewing secretly....

Do you call it dressing or do you call it stuffing?
Do you call it lovemaking or do you call it fucking?
Do you call it sexy dissection or ugly striptease or
silly slits picking at food when they should simply eat

or be eaten? At least I'm good with spicing.
At least I'm good at knifing my own wicked witch.
My bestial female flow, posing as your seasoned spill.

## Catwalk

This poem is wearing a pink leotard & shock collar.

Anonymous women voyeurs in the audience depress
buttons on handheld devices while affecting a straight face,
a blank face, a vaguely befuddled face so the poem can't pinpoint
which buzzers are placebos and which is the torture device
delivering its lesson of electrifying corrections. With dazed dismay,
this poem shapes itself into butcherbird girls. Hook-beaked and bead-eyed.

This poem is strutting down the runway with bones jutting out.
Compound fracture style. Dismembered yet still feathered,
a bridal party flocks into a catfight. This poem is ripping
rough-tongued bouquets out of thin air. Purposefully
as a high-heeled militia, the casualties apply
haute couture dressings to banged-up knees,

even though they can't recall whose altar they were kneeling at.
Falsies spill out glittered handbags. Calling cards advertise
chemical peels. This poem got burned, but is willing to try it again;
hide its epidemic nosebleed in a lipstick secret compartment.
Pretend that singe marks around the voice box are a cutting edge
necklace. Agree that mangled manikin arm roadkill is gourmet.

This poem has something to say, but it is gagging.

## Cleavage

She tilts it and sweetly scoops it—
a double dip of vanilla ice cream
with maraschino cherries on top.
She glistens it and coquettishly spills it
into so many gaping mouths
desirous to lick that, spoon that
oozing hot butterscotch

(gallivant, slink, pussyfoot)

She pin-up minxes it—
a bullet bra flaunt with peek-a-boo
lace and white satin waist-
high panties. Pearlescent girdle and garter belts.
Ornamental welts. Glazed cherry stems faked
into tiny bows and kinkier formations.
Creamy gams splayed to reveal

(stained fur, sharp burrs, bared teeth)

stiff ruffles.  A hot tease of innermost thigh.
Worm moons, counterclockwise tassels,
a tightening corset.  She looks good, but she'd look better
in a bukkake party.  Pulsing, trussed wrists, black curtain
of saturated bangs. Black flats like patent leather hooves
with coarse hair tufting.  Some kind of wild thing.
Some kind of dirty whore's heaving

(cleavage, cloven, carnage).

→

Once she is adorned by that rubber sheen thorax fetish pageant. Once her face is splatter-painted, an exquisite scene. Torn seams, hook & eye buttons busted, red-caked lips a soused sheath cum-guzzling all that throbbing meat.

Once she puts on that slaughtered animal costume, how long before he wants to drink her blood?

(Heartworm, ringworm, money shot of maggots)

**Mass Production**

1.
You can also get a tub of that size
filled with tiny debutantes. Not even talking
Cool Whip tub. Talking bigger, more durable
plastic with bright label affixed,
haphazardly stuffed with little wannabe queens,
fresh from the assembly line. That new car smell,
that pink approximation of bendable legs
under flammable dance dress. Molten plastic core.
Interchangeable whores with pose-able tiaras.

2.
The screw is rotated by a motor, feeding pellets
up the screw's grooves. The depth of the screw decreases
towards the end of the screw nearest the mold,
compressing the heated plastic. As the screw rotates,
the pellets are moved forward in the screw
and they undergo extreme pressure and friction
which generates most of the heat needed
to melt the pellets. Heaters on either side of the screw
assist in the heating and temperature control.

3.
You can also get a plastic whip, that new car friction,
pink grooves haphazardly stuffed with Cool Whip.
Of course, some of them aren't even good enough for the back seat.
The list of defects includes: blister, burn marks, color streaks, silver streaks,
de-lamination, embedded contaminants, stringiness, voids, warping,
weld lines, and splay marks. Her legs won't bend back any farther
and the nozzle hasn't even shot its load. Little wannabe whores
should bleach their assholes, the inverse of the product's shape.
Compress the heated plastic, scream like a size queen, burst into flame.

**Firecracker firecracker boom boom splatter paint**

My kitchen was suddenly invaded by egg sacks,
I mean ants, I mean egg sack antlers
like a skein of violent surrealism,

like an ouzo Ouija board fight
leading to a smothering tenterhook
then dead baby teeth affixed via paint.

You want a special treat? Here's my hot pink blender.
If you turn it on high, you'll make the eyeballs splatter
into a grade school cheerleader pom pom bad dream.

You never know what's boiling out of the girl's
locker room, but it probably involves breasts
too big and breasts too small and at the end of each
gym class, that teacher steps up and asks which
girl will stand on the stage and dance a cheer.

If nobody volunteers, then somebody's gonna be screaming
her boobs are so flat they sink into the chest,
her boobs look like another huge punching bag.

**Say she had dirty follicles**

1.
It was fine to treat her face like a thumbprint cookie
because her chest was as flat as a bisque plate
when you ripped open the bustier. Say she ripped herself.
Say she was carried away in a wet, black dog mouth.
She was passed from mouth to mouth; dark 'hood
dog to dark dog. All mangy and probably diseased.
All frothing at the mouths at the taste of her rag-
a-muffin rumpus room. Punch her in the mouth;
say you got carried away because her spit out beads,
the rank smell of her pelt. Say something unnatural
pushed you. What oozed out was the filling in a cheap
dessert product ruined with broken teeth. Say cheese.
Say shit-eating grin. Say she looked at it the wrong way.
Like a soft target. Plotting an insurrection.


2.
What you're saying is her breasts were beasts. Tried to lunge away
from her body. But that black dog deposited her at your doorstep
like a flaming sack of shit. You had to step in it, stifle that reek.
Her hellfire. Tar nation. What you're saying is her teeth
were in the wrong place. She bit you. You don't know why
you were stomping and humping both at the same time.
She tricked you. It was self defense. What you're saying is
the devil made you do it and she was the devil. Burnt
rose petals and black pepper came out. She pretended
she was bleeding. She wore a bustier made out of rat
traps. She bit and then she didn't have any teeth.

**Stubble**

I hear the blades whirring.
I hear the blades whirring.

Horripilation all over my inner thighs.
The area the depilatory missed.
Depilation failure even in the midst of my
chemical stench my meat stench lingers.

An electric carving knife. A helicopter
coming to abduct me. Dangling a meat hook
instead of a lifeline. I hear the blades

say a meat hook is my lifeline.

**Meat Chorus**

Whereupon a fleshy arrangement of sex-hungry
cellists descends upon me with their special techniques.

Straddled and packaged into cello sleeves.

I'm not a fembot. I'm not a product
like bite size sausage sliding out of cellophane sheath.
What might look like a novelty whip

is my succulent violin string warping the wood
of the cutting board. On the swinger party floor,
another instrument is the flute sculpted out of baloney.

Another greased up kisser
coming at my mouthpiece.

## Threesome

The procedure involves a 3-way mirror
and a milking machine. I'm hooked up.
I'm writhing and frothing. It's so strange
how my blue-tinged skim milk trickles out
while my reflection voluptuously pumps more
heavy cream. The triplet is strangely refined sugar
and whipping. So who are you calling

a creepy translucent woman with her milk ducts
and veins mixed up obscenely and on display?
One of me is so opaque I'm bisque triple-painted
an eggplant purple high gloss sateen. Dark lumpy moon
jellies in pipettes. Mercury in retrograde high fructose
corn syrup. Induced ovulation of metalloid beads.
My tumescent silver dragées. You could string me

multicolored and sticky around your pulsing portal
if you wanted to be risky, but you'd rather siphon me sterile.
You'd rather milk me with an automated machine.
This procedure requires a hybridization
of electrified metal suction groping flesh.
This sequence will not end very happily.
You can't soften your feelings for me.

It's another steely trap on repeat.

**Plague**

I've striven to be a silkworm,
but no matter how I maneuvered,
all that came out was stained rags,
queasy hues, too impractical
for the haute couture runway.
Another gutter ball. Another gutter ball.

Another slime ball of epic proportions.
Insectile abortions. I've tried to quell this
pink pulsating "beehive,"
but there's no stopping its gelatinous mass
production placental overdrive.
These placentas with relentless stingers.

These placentas with writhing undersides.
These placentas that were catalyzed
by high fashion eugenics. In elite back rooms,
with exotic fruit mold supreme anesthesia pump action,
they liposuctioned the secret folds of my "fat suit"
until I was exposed. My veins

housed spumes of glitter prone to misfire.
My bones were not quite good enough to boil
into consommé. Despite their ministrations,
I would never be gourmet. They inserted the speculum,
extracted the larvae. Another gutter ball.
Another awful "female creature."

## Self-Lubricating

Lovebird stuck in a sieve a terrible beating.
(He said it was because I'm a woman. He called it
an open wound.) Wings flit out my split lip.
Beaks peck through the secret fontanelle.
I've kept it veiled, but these babies are sharp
and starving. Mutant stiletto snake tongues
flicking out tissue paper (de)flowers.
I've kept it soft-spoken in words he won't grasp.
My pink cocktail umbrella is retrofitted
with poison darts, snake venom, spit of wet rats,
such bad inklings to discharge. I'm sick of blotting
my lips, holding myself back from a messy biting.

## Deer Head Variations

instead of severed, stuffed deer heads and their velvety racks,
this study is mounted with pelvic girdles with jewels
embedded in the pubis and iliac crests

the kind of jewels that might inhabit treacherous fairy tale
hair combs of the decorative and lethal bent
the kind of jewels that might adorn feminine crossbows—
hot metal & rubies & chokecherries

artificed porcelain cups contain
inexplicably wobbling eggs
although tongueless in their shells
they hum glossal murmurations

*

instead of pipe smoke plumes against a backdrop
of hunter green, stinking up the taxidermy pheasants,
this study is perfumed with a slow seep

vapors from violet veins, sugar channels, baby pears
in heavy syrup and others in formaldehyde,
glass jars of plucked feathers, bleach, honey, googly eyes,
silver-tapped wisdom teeth

these birdies are cuckoo clock quails
with crooked feet, battered beaks, askew springs
leaking out half-shattered necks,
metallic warblings cut with turpentine

*

→

as pomegranates crack open and bleed out
their pulpy seeds, she molds a small bird of marzipan
to serve as candied companion piece

or does she mean to pit the misfit birds against each other
like a scaled-down yet sinister version of a cock fight?
does she secrete snuff films into furtive vaults
as the eggs soak up pernicious vibrations, begin to convulse?

the bitter chokecherries could be itty bitty ball gags
if the eggs had mouths   if the eggs had hands
the porcelain pocills could be tiny pillories
her poison-dipped nib quivers with anticipation

\*

albumen slithers sweetly down the walls

**Mutating Cosmetic Surgery**

Kitten-heeled pinball machines ding
as gleaming eyeballs roll down chutes
of huge glitter-rouged cleavage. Clipped tails drip
a trail to the ladies room. Modified alley cats blot
oversaturated lips on stained cheesecloth.
Red wax bleeds and bleeds through pores.

Call it whatever you want as long as it's catchy,
but not too easy. Or call it too easy.
Call it a whorish gumball machine slot
and a horny hand that won't stop snaking up
until it gets caught on something sharp
that was not made to listen or let go.

When they come to your aid with the lube,
they could be a secretly perverse retail clerk
or they could be a procession of slutty nurses,
high on stilettos, volumizing mascara, oversized
rectal thermometers. Call it a sneak attack
of eyelash mites who mutate in the heat of toxic falsies.

The dissecting pan looked like a cake pan.
You could be a pinned down mouse getting screwed
in the wrong hole. If you wanted a crumb, why did you grab
at that neon glow-in-the-dark pussy billboard?
You could be a flailing pet hamster in the spiked party punch,
in the crush porn, in the rancid filling oozing out of

→

industrial-sized cheese horns. Her syringe could be breeding silicon juggernauts or subcutaneous parasites or radioactive microscopic piranha hybrids injected into your stuck pig.
She could be a leopard skin coat check girl who specializes in hooks.
She could be an 8-legged girl who wants to Ziploc® them around you and patent a new sex move called the Futuristic Jello® Mold

that ends with her squeezing out plastic eggs spring loaded with bloody yolks and flesh tone nylons. Call it golden brown spawn trapped inside a bouncy ball, a curvilinear prison of artificial candy-colored swirls. Call it a multi-hued hussy hugged by layers of vulcanized rubber. A wet dream that morphs into a nightmare that morphs into a reality TV show.

*As the officer approached, he thought it was a mannequin that had been set on fire.* Call it a guinea pig fiberglass skin graft that leaves us scooping burnt sugar into body bags.
A botulism baby could rise up from the melted down cellulite.
We could handcuff her, stuff her in a pillow sham, tap her dollie crème brulee with a gleaming scalpel.

**Ladyfingers**

What do you get when you mix one woman's
personality disorder with 3000 pounds of thrust?
If you insert a hot baked apple dumpling into the crotch
panel of a pair of black pantyhose and swing? Ladyfingers
crawl out the holes in their heads and festoon the whole
room with cheesy frosting. She never liked the sour cream
layer on her bite size cheesecake. She looked so dis-
embodied after waxing. The hideous heft of her naked
white quivering goiter, or was that another giant egg?

\*

She never liked the way they seeped before she
cracked them open on the edge. She looked so dis-
enchanted when they all started crawling away.
A steamy latte is the sign of a typical teen. Paper doll
body with carrier pigeon wings. Meanwhile her coffee is cold
fusion oviduction with end result voluptuous prostheses.
They don't want any of those dregs going down their throats.
She packs a lunch: thermos full of raw wieners and the little slot
in the lunch box is a gingerbread girl in a confessional booth.

\*

One mantra could be "treat not treatise," except it's not
menacing enough for she who was born in a claw machine
lined with stuffed tripe. Maybe if she lost half her body
weight, she'd stop laying eggs and spitting hungry lice.
"Having mouthparts adapted for sucking" sounded good
to them until she actually started sucking. She looked so dis-
ingenuous when their steamy filling was drooling out of her
elongated tart. It's what's inside that counts. Under her dress,
that gingerbread girl is praying mantis mandibles under duress.

**Domestic Disturbance**

Douse tongue in scalding herbal tea. Breach.
Yellow onions un-paper themselves. I lob
a soft body into the stew pot.

Through watery eyes, this is such a pretty
little nuthouse. Spin through the empty red
pistachio shells, black walnuts, candied pecans,

sugared almond slivers inserted underneath fingernails
until my knees buckle into a plié. Oh pantaloon-atic!
Oh washboard! Oh breastbone beneath which fungal

fruiting bodies breed. Into the stew pot, the butternut
squash twitching as if against an electric fence. The angry red
welts in my wrist. The bloodsuckers drained

my heirloom tomatoes. The husks in my drawers;
the crotch panel stained with a soupçon of beef broth.
Oh soupçon! I signed the contract! I signed on the dotted line

like cutting coupons, like julienned beets, like a wickerwork
basket of battered pointe shoes. A constellation of tiny blood stains
against pink sateen backdrop, but now I have bare feet.

Glass splinters into the stew pot, pantiliners into the stew pot,
antifungal cream, delousing powder, bleach.
Empty the stew pot into the laundry machine;

turn on the spin cycle. Sing a little pretty ditty
about a fruitcake with gangrene. Oh heaving bear claw!
Oh raw crescent roll! It's bedroom time, my dearies.

My doll-hole is drilled to sweet dimensions.
My blow-hole is spouting cream. I'm a little teapot;
hear me scream. My hard-bodied manikin hovers above

my scene; such a tease before it crashes.
Torpedo torso splintering. Subdermal plummeting.
Fiberglass shards into the dumpling box.

## Snake in a Can Gag

1. Oh Darlingtonia, secrete your nectar for me. Oh lewd mucilage.
Oh fleshy funnel cake. Your nectar bribe is laced with poison.
Your forked tongue leaf is purplish-green and beckons me
to dip another finger into your translucent false exit.

*

2. I wanted to stick my hand down the garbage disposal.
Right before the roller coaster plummeted downhill, I wanted to
grab the scaffolding. I wanted to snap necks, cut veins, throw poison
darts inappropriately. Desire is sometimes rooted in sick compulsion.
Desire is sometimes strangled by twisted consumption. I wanted
to give you something different. Serve you up mangled flesh.

*

3. I dispatched my rabid flock of killer carrier pigeons posthaste.
"Bring me back his gonads, girls!" said I
& so they did, compressed into their little silver leg vials.
When I took off the lids, the harvested penis sprang out
like the snake in a can gag. "That gives mixed nuts a new meaning,"
I laughed to my exotic flock of carrion pigeons. They advanced.

*

4. They may occasionally catch small vertebrates such as rats and lizards
& bestow in bite-size pieces upon my porch or under my pillow.
They can seal the lobes hermetically and form a specialized stomach.
Sometimes I think of my special birds as each made up
of a central ovary and two wings on either side.

**Venus Tree**

I planted my oranges with teeth.
I offered my crush a piece of spiked fruit;
next thing I knew, he was missing an arm.

Could this be transcendence in a new-fangled way
or were we just consuming each other? How do we
move past our mutilation into our desired sweet bite?

Forbidden to talk about hunger, we suffer
involuntary movements of the tongue—
weevils, vowels, forking out.

My tongue flicking, my limbs twitching
like orange-splotched salamander tails.
I wanted to chew and swallow, but I spewed it—

a bloody spume of glitter dripping down.

**Saint Lucy Eyes**

1. Martyr mouths to be filled and then stomped on
body parts to be pried open poured into
choked gagged dragged stabbed left for dead
who cares they're just objects with holes

2. Dredged out suppurated glitter head
pull off all the legs of that daddy long legs
stick the un-moveable circle in a shot glass
until it dies into a tiny eyeless skull
or a disembodied eye to be inserted
into an empty slot, another ripped out hole

3. If you just add water it might rise up and grow
new eyes and open them, until you shove it back down
into the hot poison cauldron and watch

Purple brain flowers burst out

## 3. Gradually Ebbing Down — (Para)Normal Uncertain Wives

**Semiabstract Self Portrait**

My red yarn runs across
the floor like a bleeding rat.

My neck veins stick out
further and further
until they start dripping down.

Fans cannot trap me
because I don't have any fans.
Only my own mind is allowed
to hang from this ceiling,
drip, drop, and dangle
over the edge.

My disembodied logic floats faster
around the room, trying
to fill every spoon with non

liquid sinking into
confetti bones.

**Ghost Teeth**

Little white floaters in my field.
More ghost eggs for the loony bin.
Telekinetic embryo, a lingering wet kiss
like electrodes to the wrist.

Sometimes I feel like a lamb chop marionette.

My bones cold inside their raw dress.
More ghost insinuations like parasites
that gnaw flesh. What would happen if I just snipped
the sides of this enclosure? If I just refused

to cook myself today? No matter how doughy,
I know there's blood inside. My underside.
My small basket of ragamuffins dares you
to take another invisible bite.

Sometimes I feel like swing dancing with a meat cleaver.

**Parasitic Twin**

A dark ghost key inserts itself
into a dark ghost ignition.
Dark as in can't comprehend
the specific delineations
of the interlocking parts,
but sometimes hear
the sudden click. Others,

it's more of an amorphous sound.
More of a jittery insinuation.
More of an oily slinkiness.
A motor an uneven rev
in a tattered throat.
Pluralized throats.
Pleurisy throats. A dark ghost

with many cockeyed heads,
the wormy kittens come out.
Small, patchy army of bedlam.
Scritching, scraggling, scrabbling,
festering scabs on their undersides,
milk lust in their eyes. Some bulging,
some slits. Some pinworms squiggling.

Some pinholes where something tried to affix
to poster board, but they weren't good
poster children. They weren't anybody else's
art project. They were mine.
I poked holes to try to drain them,
but they just bubbled up into more
ghost ignitions. They are mine,

→

but they don't come when called.
They come whenever they want to.
When they come I have to balance
rickety dishes of spoiled milk upon
precarious ledges. I have to pose
rancid scraps of cottage ham,
plumply peeking out of netting.

I won't say their names aloud.
I won't hand feed them, but I do
have to watch them lick my sick
offerings with diseased tongues
and diseased tongues get stuck
in a notch. In a dark ghost ignition
in a lobe. I have to watch them ruin

another failed attempt to write them off.
Another deformity is pinworms stream out
the whole time the motor is running and I can't
stop thinking rev and shiv make a good off rhyme
until shiv is replaced with handfuls of bodkins.
Another deformity is the claws never retract.

## The New Witchery

Burnt lace wrapped around mouse bones.
Violet pastilles clamped inside skeletal
bird beaks. Mounds of wretched doll meat
to be melted down. That mealy-mouthed slut
with her Mons Venus heat must be made
to hold nettles and burrs on her tongue.
Steeped burls is the new tea, chilling and darkening.
Damp moss is the new fur, crawling with tiniest fauna.
That girl begged to serve as art model, as canvas
for the new witchery. The latest hair color is PEAT BOG.

It skitters like spider feet when you rip open
the black tasseling that sewed her lips into a snarl
until you were ready for her to speak. Now she's your silk-lined clutch
with decorative beading. Her knotty maw. Her rotten zinnias bleeding.
You fill her raw mouth-hole with dark purple votive. You make her drip
wax when she whimpers. You make her flicker on and off
like some haunted fixture. The latest hair color is SPLIT PEA SOUP,
spilling into spittle-flecked milieu. Before it sputters,
you use her flame to plant a catalyst kiss
into the furrowed scalp of a dirty manikin head.

Sowed her lips into dark tendrils
writhing from the new root beds.

**The Ugly Duckling**

One half a doll swath; the other half unruly. This is my dirty-feathered fate. Birthed of the black swan lace, a high-pitched soprano solo of my past, but my present is loose gravel, is groveling. No longer can I make my diaphragm work that way; that heave that smooths into sweet syllabics. My new rhythm spurts and gags.

**The Moth**

A beating inside a rocking horse. Rickety wood with splinters, flaking paint, strange bulge like an eyeball trying to escape. Coming unglued between the legs, my moth light flickering. My red mass splitting into spectral wings, flitting against a bare bulb.

**The Swan**

Their sound bites are fake swan songs. I need a whirring, serrated beak like electric knife through generic feathers. Talk about a pillow fight! When my mangled swan explodes out of the can someone will probably ask if it's some kind of balloon animal, but since when do balloon animals have bloody feathers? Or feathers? Or blood?

**The Sugar Glider**

If the sugar glider turns into a dreamboat, then that means the drowning has begun. It's not dancing; it's dying. As some kind of defense mechanism, you think, 'Sink or float, you furry little witch.' Maybe because its sodden wing span resembles a dark cape.

**Dead Raven**

you came tapping, tapping

typography of dead beak
of missing feather ink
of small empty sockets

velvet violet lining

peck and pluck and peck and
pluck and coo and pluck and
coo not a stilt, not a swallow, not a lovebird

the velvet sinking

the tiny heart seizing up as I encircle
fragile neck bones with my fingers
thread through your new armature

into the chamber

your bones are hollow flutes
your bones are tapered syllables
of longing for the bijous that used to be your eyes

nevermore

**The Pig Box**

gaping piglet maw
glutted with wilted posy
of plucked-from-stem Antirrhinum
malformed confetti

the mouth-zone exhibits
distended blue
stretched balloon aesthetic
the rest of her is painted

anodized bronze
with one pink strip
traversing the underside
little whore slit

pleasingly plump
corn-fed porker
crotchless panties
in a metal box

snapdragon flaccid mouths
won't make a sound anymore
stuffed inside another mouth
rouge gorge gag

mouth within mouth muteness
sweet postmodern muzzle
dead flowers to muffle her
occlude the oinking tongue

→

jaw-flapping coven cloy
cloven-hoofed teat-freak
painted lady corpse coy
hussy with her pink peek

of rigor mortised meat
wired neatly into place
dilated throat
sticky silk sate

of many smaller throats
collapsed into limp bouquet
tilt her for the grand finale
orifice spills soundless pink stamen

**A Song**

When the straight pins curve into your swallow,
you will die starlet. An opera star vocal pierced through
poison-dipped feathers. A poison soaked through
long buttoned gloves. A poison soaked through
contorted neck inside out. A lush dripping boa.

Tiny cinderblocks tied to your swallowtails,
dragging down under dark water. A trawl
as the wing beats slow, just before they choke
into a soft corpse no bigger than a guttural vowel
lodged in a velvet-lined coffin of throat.

Haunted core. Haunted corridor of pin pricks,
of torn netting, of pill box veil, of swallow wail
swallow wail swallow wail swallow wail....

**Sieve**

This lambkin is sheared and encased in ice.

When the violet pastilles cut into
its tongue, its blood felt like blue frosting;
its mouth was a candied frostbite.
Dark veins in a cave. Glazed sugar cane.

The chilly ditties of icing piped out
witches, rosettes, witches. Silver platter pedestal
for ice sculpture malediction. Design of black stitches
traversing the underside where the blanket of cold chenille

tried to fit snugly, but was bladed away.
Exposure, powdered sugar, exposure. Gelid hooves
cobbled in icy peach cobbler. With frozen pits
of eyes stuffed with preservative fur, this could be a bog lamb,

but it is a shorn lamb, a tundra lamb, a glacier lamb.
A clot of not quite edible marzipan stuck under a rigid tongue.
When will it melt into sugared witch sounds? When will it drown
into pits of blue slush, blindfolded by a sticky strip of silver rosettes?

## The Paper Dolls

The paper dolls gave me this dream. A frozen wedding cake the next year. A deep freezer-burned slab with ruffles & swirls. Some hard little kernels to swallow. Some hard little kernels to lodge in the corners of teary eyes. Obstructed ducts may require this poultice: measure raw kernels of rice and lavender buds into a small silk bag. Concentrate on ribbon ties. Concentrate on words like desire and flexuous. Concentrate on cake freshly baked. Don't feel sorry for the paper dolls trapped inside that sorry piñata. Loosen your velvet ribbon, beat the papier mache, let their bodies spill forth and float. Wherever they land, bury them beneath kernels and buds. If they have linked hands, use sewing scissors. If they try to elicit your sympathies by bleeding, recognize this as part of the dream. Realize that cake crumbs are thicker than blood. The surface of paper can be changed.

***

The paper dolls are shuffling
like self-possessed playing cards.
The paper dolls are shuffling
like other-possessed paper zombies.
They are dipping into skim milk,
then spreading violet-scented talc
to disguise their off-color aromas.

Yes, they are disintegrating.
Yes, they are reanimating—
forcing themselves through mesh;
emerging new strains in the basin.
The paper dolls are insinuating
fictive little personhoods;
tiny grappling hooks into flesh.

→

They are mucking up my surface.
If I'm the cratered moon on a dark night,
then they are wearing murky gray
astronaut suits sown from owl pellets.
Having already rummaged through
my wastepaper basket, their gluey tongues
are licking my tights into quivering tripe.

They want me to blubber; then they want to
disappear into my folds, so they can't be folded
into scraplings of see-through rice paper. Mere
kernels. I've tried to tell them they are obsolete
love letters. oooooooo o o o o o o  o o o o   O  O  O
P.S. A thin gruel of blood is drooling out of one
paper doll's mouth piece.  Please RSVP.

\*\*\*

The paper dolls cakelike, too many eggs, high altitude baking instructions and I'm feeling sorry again. How could I have fallen for this feigned blood sisterhood? How could I have fallen for this cold compress? Due to contractions, contradictions, contraindications, I don't wish to say thank you for the envelope that contained a prescription, but I will say thank you for the envelope that contained a light blue rectangle, which may or may not be a piece of sky. I can almost see the ghostly outline of another paper doll floating by, which is not meant to insinuate angelhood. I wish she was a paper-thin, girl-shaped hot air balloon, bearing my heart in her flame-powered basket. Carrying my heart up, steamy contraband to next destination.

**Haunted Sea Urchin**

It may go for long periods without food.
It is way too spiny to hold inside
where it lies dormant then suddenly turns on
its constellation of glowing photospheres.
Tiny spotlights revolve around me
as I collapse onto an unstable stage.
I thought she would sink not float.

I spill like prickers in vitreous fluid.
She spills like blue-green light from a fish
that lives deep under water. I thought it
would float down not up like glowing bile.
I thought it would settle at the bottom
until the bones were smoothed, until the flesh was digested
into tiny plankton and krill. Intestinal flora.

She unfathomably surfaces again, her skeleton
even sharper, her wedding dress of plant and animal scraps,
swimming towards me, a phantasmagoria
of photosynthesized tongues darting
my elastic stomach, tincturing my wet eyes
with tainted bioluminescence. What if
my sodden head is a carnivorous sponge?

Red-tinged saltwater makes stiff casements
out of silk pillowcases. Krill kill bed bugs.
It may go for long periods without sleep.
It is way too deep to contain
these clots of algae in my sockets.
I cough up weedy sea dragons like cryptic,
beautiful aliens. Their fins stop humming,

but their mouths keep foaming inside
my own foaming mouth until my life goes blind.

**Giant Squid**

Maybe I won't die because his first wife did, something to do with ratios, probability. Not that I could ever understand those so-called proofs or anything else mathematical,

but I'm in tune with underwater jet propulsion, rhythms of pulsing tentacles. Something invades a natural habitat with a misguided statistical inference or am I feeling

paranormal interference? Maybe she wants me to succumb to suction cups imprinting their circular scars, stained with dark ink. Sharp, finely serrated rings.

Wedding rings. Maybe she wants me to give something; to cross over with her love letters, to cross over with her what ifs. A gelatinous material holds them together;

all these eggs are punctured, but none of them drained. Interior a dunk tank teeming with the giant squid and me seated precariously above it. Throw the first rock.

**Hydra**

Voice box more weedy than reedy.
Water snakes carry me down to dredge
and almost always poisonous. All this silt.
Sea sponges wrapped in leeches. An opening
surrounded by tentacles. Baby hydrae clamp
onto hyacinth. I can make them detach
and free-float until they clamp again. Sucker punch.
Hydra, hydraulic, hydrocephalic. Something to sink
its teeth, something to suck out the toxins,
something to spit the toxins into another hole.

## Another Medusa

She self-enforces a temporary muteness.
A trick in which her tongue unroots from its dank cave.
A misshapen sea anemone out of its element
until she sends it back underwater to quietly undulate;
to swell, to lengthen, to regenerate.

When you struggled against her, she mistook
those death throes for pleasure. A cloying clam adorned
by filth-encrusted barnacles and poison glands
as you drowned in the moat of her throat.
Scratch that anemone. It was more

like baby eels forced through a funnel
into a small orifice. Or a venomous sea snake
insinuating itself between your lips, repeatedly
flicking that wet tongue like a salt lick instinct gone sinister.
You saw yourself pulling it out by the root, dripping.

You saw it writhing even after it was removed.
A trick in which she only pretended to be desirous
of your measured stylus strokes. You were nothing more
than a blot of punctuation at the end of a sinuous sentence.
She has enough black ink to spill herself, to be disastrous,

to gorge herself. Her dangling threads engorged into
pulsating tentacles. The suction cups engaged your hand
then elongated into fangs. Her triangular head became a messy tangle
of hissing snakes. She was nothing more than a vise grip slime case
seeking to envenomate. How does a lover suck that poison out?

**Volary**

How was it planted, this fir tree
growing inside a human lung?
He hacks up blood and seeds.
Then a bird with rarefied nettles in its beak.

She dreams the sweet sculpting of wings
on butter birds. A glint of ice birds
with rapt half-lives. What kind of birds
pop out their chests, glazed trickles,

rolls fresh from an oven, gorgeous signature
biscuit, clot of mangled feathers, encircling each
other, sticky as baklava. Our ribs are honey-drenched
catacombs. Our hearts are small bogs.

**seamstress of the belly of the beast**

Prickly thorns may be an intricate latticework
wrapped around a secret luminaria.
Glowing frog throat, swelling bird egg, lilting
warbler feathers alight. I don't want to snuff it,
but sometimes it burns my tongue.

A tiny blue heron floats in hot buttered rum,
then throbs into a blue-black Hieronymus Bosch scene.
From delicate origami nestling to flaming paper wings,
veiny beak. Oily clots of dark paint bleed
through pores and test my seams.

Let me rip open a little. Maybe I can stitch myself
together in new ways. Let me rip open all the way.
I'll entrust someone with my collection of gleaming
needles and threads. My desire to be unleashed.

**Purple Speculum**

Make me your feather-spread saint. Halo me
in a torrent of legerdemain erasures on ripped out paper.
Beak, beak, beak until I am tizzy with new imprints.
My ruffled underside. My plucked spine. My peeled skin
a browning apple dumpling under your spoon.
I'm such an ugly duckling. A darling of grime-cake
ventricle erotica. Neurotica flung up against a plate
glass window and pumped full of your filthy
filthy filthy filthy filthy filthy. Berate my borderline
personality. Martyr me, swan song me, duck pond me.
Tranquilize me and then slam me up against your fountain of blood.

**Volatility**

My moon is a poisonous zoo garden brimming with bizarre erotica. Like vile flasks, these coagulating feet clip off dark red cloud bursts between the knees; split blood drenched toenails like parasitic parasails.

Watch this sloe gin sideswipe seep into you like a storm surge. Feel night vision sparklers drip black raspberry out my borderline holes. Rip out another love song drenched with doppelganging bad lands.

My squirmy heart star-lets are about to explode from outer space like a strange photo booth tainted with biohazards. Shove another lethal dose down this throbbing throat until my cracked pinholes undulate and mutate into slithering tentacles. Nothing can contain this hissing monsoon.

Butterfly valves plunged between my bio-luminescent thighs; throttled them into blue lipped sea kraits.

**Coiled**

Love masks overtook me.
(What is real love?)

Brain scan brain scan brain scan.
Spider eggs ready to burst.

Spray paint brimming with tiny eggs
separating into discolored legs.

Desire dissipated. Colorful bite marks
poisoned pieces of me.

## 4. Suddenly Ebbing Down Deeper — (Ab)Normal Waves on the Brink

**dream about being**

dream about being kicked out too fast

the hospital bed speeding and turning me
into nothing. mom keeps trying to call me
hello, hello, juliet, where are you?
but i can't answer. i'm nobody

"I'm nobody! Who are you?
Are you — ..."

a hole that can't speak
for itself anymore,
a sudden feeding tube
inserted with surgical scalpel

little broken scissor blades,
cutting me into disheveled pieces,
ripped out strands falling farther away
everyone else is off in the distance

i am alone and do not know
what is going on. am i dead
and nobody cares? am i
alive but expiring?

where am i going? am i
still part of me or am i almost gone,
but stuck inside an uncontrollable
breathing machine, nothing but
a mechanical corpse vat,
nothing but an ongoing unspeaking

dream about being nobody

**Marmalade Glaze**

Like a terrible pterodactyl necklace it bit,
sunk in and left me
bloody. Snorted thousands
of remembered words out of my system.
Appealing turned into appalling.

**Red Shrink Wrap**

My hands are staple removers with metal fangs. Blown up promotional balloons are now bloody crullers, misplaced phalli, bulbous sausages ready to burst out their conjoined links. That soap dispenser was a disconnected appendage, then it was an entire cow, placidly chewing its cud, now it is a bright red tooth, leaking. Dark push pins through my brain.

**Mauvette Maroon**

*Many household objects can be the basis of amusing puppets.* They haven't lived until they've eaten a chocolate-covered painkiller hybrid.

It filled my lips with villiform wigs.

Hair hard to swallow without strangling my heart. The bittersweet root of it is black licorice stuck to a fiberglass skull.

**Angioplasty Show**

Tiger teeth exhale red angiosperms
like a tattered face mask.
Misshapen corpse vat writhes open
a dark vaudevillian synapse.

**Crepuscular Creep**

Impalement arts with fang shapes and furry lumps
like some kind of bloody parachute silk clotting between teeth
like odd rats scurrying in & out of debris, laughing
like little gray witches attacking my marbled brain

Reptilian glitter stuck inside a strange crematorium

## Arterial Discombobulation

1.

Slip-gaps vs. slit-gasps.
I don't want to be a weak shell casing,
a broken stained crème brulee,
an irrational shape shifting bog.
Blobbing, clotting, throbbing pupa strangulation.
What if poisonous insects live inside my veins?
What if my carotid arteries are predatory beasts?
What if they wish to slaughter my entire neck;
impale me? Was that a bodily tremor or
a body bag streamer?


2.

What might be sticking out my neck,
bursting forth from my discolored throat,
and what if it explodes? Am I wrong,
misshapen, on the brink of another dissection?
Will I lose another lover, more power? What if
my whole personality gets impaled? What if
I can no longer walk, talk, dance, kiss, speak for myself,
read, or write poetry? What if I lose all my passion, lust,
interest and love?  What if another artery bleeds out
until it removes the real me?

### Broken Blister Pearls

Folded in on myself and heavy-lidded,
the heat is unbearable.

My contortion is hinged legs,
singed hair, doll voice rattling
like charred marbles stuck behind the trapdoor
of a throat that used to be so musical,
so flexuous. So sweet-skinned

in my sequined acrobat dress and feathered masquerade mask.
I perfectly purled across laminated stages.
I lightly tumbled through flaming gold hoops
and white balloons without bursting,
without melting down.

Now the antique music box motif
is imprinted on my fevered forehead.
Folded in on myself and heavy-lidded,
this box is too small I can't breathe.
Bones creak like sick swallow song.

My contortionism is twisted swan neck,
blistering. Beak bound shut with burnt ribbon.
White feathers disappear into acrid poofs
as the music box motor winds down;
scritches out the last few rusty notes—

bird vertebrae, cauterized syllables, crushed vowels.
Now I'm so small I could sift through
the tiny gold hoop of an earring.
Now I'm so small I'm hardly a handful
of ash from a pair of scorched pointe shoes.

**Cremains of a smoldering pirouette,
bedecked with blood-stained baby teeth.**

## The Fortune Teller

1.

Faceted glass glints from the ceiling. Chrysalides quiver
from lead crystal. Cryptic revelations are her pets.
'The flowers weep and the Gothics feed,' she purrs.
Her lips like dark orange burns posed theatrically
around a burr. A rusty embouchure. Waxy debris
staining the choppers. Her voice like cocoa pod husk,
carnival squash, grotesque curves of a dried gourd rattling, rattling....
Some days I am hollow. Some days I am filled with bright pulp.
An uncarved pumpkin ridden to the top
of a roller coaster, held by swaying stem. A cremaster.

2.

The skin begins to peel off. There is every danger.
It attaches itself to the silk pad by its last pair of false legs
and hangs head down. Being a delicate bag of fluid,
it will crash to death. To stay at one place fixed and safe,
a cremaster is twisted several times and screwed firmly.
It consists of a bulb with hundreds of hooks or barbs.
When this bulb is thrust into the silk pad,
the hooks get locked up with the silk threads.
Rapid convulsions occur along the size of a small button.
'Will you fasten or unfasten what dangles by a thread?'

**Mortuary Cabinet**

Something so wet and meaty
should not have rasped out
that skittering away sound
as if it was on its way to being gone.
Then I was left with slithery arms,
with bristly hair between the teeth
of a fine-tooth comb that was
not fine enough for me to keep.

I am so much smaller—a peeled grape
submerged in old lady perfume.
Awful dousing, broken divining rod,
a sickly-sweet cyanotic rigor.
My tale used to be so very soft.
Now stiff blue tissue bleeds out
creepy old church organ music
when I raise the scalpel.

Like a corkscrew too broken to open
a bottle of red wine, I have to shatter.
Watch it seep too fast to soothe my rattling throat.
My sound is like shrapnel in the heart (or a tiny seed).

**Love Can Be a Chokecherry**

It starts with a multi-colored glitter dress lifted up high
to show thighs wrapped with garter belts
made out of garter snakes.

She knows they're not poisonous, but
she finds out they're not really big enough
for her own magnetized thighs, unless she sits still
in one place forever. It's a cold place, especially at night.

She knows another nightmare is coming
when the bird sounds turn into dark moans.
Mounds of wings torn, ripped, pitched
until she wonders when did wings even exist?

None of this is real, so why give birth to more?
Somebody will sea the shells, but not the birds,
tiny fetuses stuck on concrete, dripping beaks,
ants crawling in and out of the cracked necks.

Now they deserve to be hung from a tree
like rotten chokecherries. Like broken ornaments
that will fall down hard, finally trash themselves
into oblivion, then be flung into the cesspool.

It starts with a kiss that turns into a rotten apple chokehold.
Being smothered into nothing.
A bitten into, spit out core.

**Red Moon Ashes**

Red moon tonight; red rag
doll eyes.  As soon as she rises up
into brightness again, she turns
dark again.  Ashes, ashes, she hideously
writhes and grotesquely whirrs; another
misshapen blood drenched dis-
aster of ash writhing from her
legs until she has no real footing left.
Red toenails like sharp stars fall down fast
and who could possibly catch & hold
all this mess?  Who would want to
bite into a bloody broken bird egg?

## Red Lunatic

Loony bin pyrotechnics glimmer
inside my disaster zone, call me
a new sort of sizzling underwater forensic science;
what will you find deep down here?
Will red fins bramble or writhe open

a snake hissing into Bloodybelly Comb Jelly?

I tried to turn burn marks into sticky drizzles
but my whip-poor-will songs oozed out red pussy
willow nightmares. I did not wish for red devil centers
with the last of the turquoise eggs falling out, cracking.
My wisdom teeth never grew to replace those holes.

**Blue Marriage**

What made me think there was only one color of endless blue?

Sweet blue fruit congealed into a blue blood bath,
colder and colder, how
do frozen blood clots sing?

Maybe from the radio inside
a car in the middle of a blue demolition derby
until it crashes and dissolves.

Is it dissolution or poisoned discord,
if I keep trying to extract myself
from cracked handles? Screeching

inside my head, but I'm trapped
in a bad dream and the words won't emerge
in real life. A stuck tongue keeps breaking

the mirror and kookaburra sits in the old gum tree
between frigid blue branches with no more leaves
until the broken holes turn into a cruel Chupacabra—

something that might not really exist.
Maybe my song never did, but I can still hear it
soundlessly groaning, dripping down into discolored blue.

Love is the color of dead blue skin silently screaming.

## 5. Off & On Flow – Almost Drowning, But Then Resurging

**Why I Dye My Hair Red**

While drinking a Bloody Mary, I think I almost died.
Is that puke, blood, or did I just spill
my glass before I passed out?
All I know is when I woke up,
the whole floor was covered in red
and I was alive again, but forever haunted.

Inside my head, sharp glass flies around the room
and won't stop spilling out fast. I'm silently screaming
inside my head, don't drop me, don't drop me,
but they always do, fall down and break
when I'm awake and fly when I'm asleep,
and suck the red out of my hair again.

Spit the top of my head down on the floor.

**Sucker Punch**

My lolly suddenly splintered into glass,
sharp but tiny points of chartreuse,
broken knife blades. An extra-sticky shiv.

I glimmered then tongue lashed
bloody gags. A crying jag so long my tear
streaks needled all the way down.

The brain swerves remain the same but the face ages.
Even the mouth's butter cream is now retching out
a wrecking zone wrench. A slow taper down in pitch

will drastically crack. A screaming siren will lose
her voice then turn her own head into a grotesque gorgon.
Who would want to bite into Miss Havisham's

wrinkles or lick her stale cake hole disaster zone?
A dissecting tray filled with mildewed desecration
will not make anybody swoon, until my beheading.

**Vintage Pom Pom Underwater**

It glitters and glows and then explodes.

A mummified octopus looks like a broken balloon
who suddenly turned old. Half the suckers
slashed by scissor blades. Black blood bath
filled my nosebleed dreams until my mouth dripped
and dried. Flung out fast, no longer wet.

Hard haunted rocking horse head, repeatedly swaying
forward and back, forward and back in the same space,
unable to fly, but starting to break between my thighs.
Frayed edges, face wedges in between cracking mirrors.

Bruised legs, banged up nose, sizzling fire cracker skin dying,
unstable middle-aged mind affixed to tainted cheerleader body.
(I was never a cheerleader in real life. I was never popular in real life.
What is real? Why am I sinking down under these misshapen rafters?)

This frazzled costume is a short reminder of ongoing flow and ebb.
How I never get the moves right until it's too late.
How the bright stains around my eyes darken
and shift into wrinkles. I'm sinking down inside
my own tiny body bag again. Alone alone alone.

A bloody little pom pom in formaldehyde.

**Contorted Impregnation**

An unexpected seizure crashed me into the fire pit;
burned my face into embered grotesque.
Screamed the blazing light, "You want
to keep thinking you're not so hot? Now you are."

For a long time my gaze was swallowed down
under the glaze vat. Overpainted and hidden
until the bloated Ophelia bulbed out from between
my thighs; brewed a conjoined nuthatch.

Faces writhing like strobe lights; gleaming red
bird twins dangling pools of blood. Pole dancing three ways
with three legs in jam jar shape. Ripped out
eye holes spew the laughing gas.

**Drain Potion**

If you try to turn me into a mangled, hairless manikin head, I will know you're unaware of the spangled shape shifting maneuvers I can throw. It might not happen fast, but I can grow

my own drowned hair into spiral shapes; into semi-circle poison beautyskull lollipops. Then one day when you stick your fingers down the drain, oh beware of my new spectral writhing

which will suddenly shimmy and plunge themselves deep inside your neckline, your mouth, your eyes—hack one of those babies out and replace it with my haunted drain head art.

**My sorrow is not something you can eat**

I've tried to turn gag streaks into plumage;
my wings pinhole, canopies spew
undulating horror through lilac flanks.

Blood drenched mishmash; manikin panic pricks
instead of fingers; noggin a gruesome dis-
aster zone. Such deep brambles can't be
contained. Who can eat out a crotched gray

brain coalesced with tubes of splatter paint?
Who can swallow a sinking down froth of inky oblivion?
Who can unravel cold inundation into a new glisten?

**Insecticide Dye Job**

Nobody else can keep you inside them long enough to glue you back together. Nobody wants to anyway. Nobody desires to dye your strands together and dive into your revolting mess. Nobody will stick to the different ways you tension thread your own head and then call its damage unfathomable and claim you are repeatedly dive bombed with insect stings. As if every new set of wings is bound to break and diverge towards poison aimed at your head. Aimed straight but then warped into another spewed bottle of broken repellant. Nobody can hear your buzz flair. Your dye looks more purple inside the shower than it does on your dark hair, but nobody wants to take a shower with you.

Even if you would shave it all off for them. Even if you tell them it's the only time they can see all of you with your panties off, because you don't want the insects to crawl inside that part too. As soon as you tell him he can keep it inside you all night (forever), he will pull it out and let the stinging insects invade (forever). They always pull out too soon or not soon enough. Now you're an upset; now you're pregnant with another swarm of confusion. Now you're just a hole filled with nothing except your own contorted head.

Your head is an unfocused spew factory, from purple blood bath to insects launching inside your vagina, swerving your hives into carnage. In and out of that ramped up high voltage dye cut vibe. Your lips are sealed with ram rods, when all you really wanted was to try something real. When that failed to work, you tried to settle into a non-human device, but the sex toy turned off too. Turned into fang shapes hissing inside your lips, all around your hips. Piercing under your bangs and then deep inside you.

→

After ripping it out of your drip dying hair, you will need to write out another sign to place above the toilet, so when they see those red blobs on the seat, they don't think it is menstrual blood. It's from everything around you turning insectile, biting in and spewing out cracked eggs filled with stinky detritus. They poison you and then pull themselves out. You rip out more and more of your own debris and flush it partway down and then pull it back out of the clogged drain and try to decide what the hell to name it. A bulgy eyed red rabbit hole with viscera inside until it goes blind. Malformed black sheep tongues. Black holes in between another sharp stream of rampant purple spikes.

**How Many Holes Can You Handle?**

1. Too many holes might turn you
into a black lagoon with poison
swimming inside you. What if he tells you
he's thinking about your tits,
you in a witch hat, going down
into a lake that keeps sinking?


2. At the bottom, pearl sacs rip open,
blisters burst under the tongue. A blustering
blastosphere spell of passion might shoot out
of the water at a breakneck pace, but oddly twisted.
It will rip flesh off the bottom of your legs.


3. You're a waitress dress with skull legs affixed.
Red spiders crawl up and down your thighs.
Half and half, slightly sweetened coffee
or black? Is it sugar or poison drip drip
dripping out your eyes? Is it an iris
or a multicolored wormhole?

**Spew**

I turn ghostly spitting up
molten vinyl from haunted maws.

My eyeballs lilt towards ceiling fans,
machinated screwballs of disorder/

desire to elongate, trigger a socket,
reactivate my glottal snags.

**Spawning**

I will turn my brain paralysis into art.
I will rip off my hanging nails; replicate
with poison-induced ginger snap fervor.

My carotid a fusion of baroque and grotesque—
rococo starfish arms oozing out spore glitter.
Swooning into cold/hot water non-solubility.

I will turn my writhing legs into jelly
fish donut hole arterial chartreuse
shaking machines. On, off, on.

## Viral Spiral

Charm School torched,
rabid rivulets sift from my paws.
Scarred, scared, but not stiff.
Who do they think I am?

I used to be pornographic eggs oozing from fruitcake.
Then I got flung into a snoring saw mill.
My mammoth splinters barbed out;
could not be devoured.

Even if partly disembodied, I cannot be severed.
I will not be formless. Even if I am convulsing,
seeping what looks like parasites in a scissor
stabbing nightmare. Except I am not parasitic.

I am skittering marrow in between distortion.
Soon to burst forth from beastly twisting;
salivating my own salvation.
Pink forks of finely-tuned fury.

**Un-sided Self Portrait**

My red yarn brings all the boys to the yard
and then sinks them down under the buoys.

My dark crystals are hidden inside
sunken ravens.

Just because I sink down
doesn't mean I still can't swim
in my own directions.

Doesn't mean I still can't maneuver up.
Maybe I just don't want to
with you.

Some of you take sides too quickly,
as if there are only two.
I'm a many-sided protrusion.

Sometimes I like to keep
the positive parts to myself
and only release the negatives.

I can sink myself, keep my own
glitter under wet ashes,
until I decide to rise it up.

## About the Author

Juliet Cook has been writing poetry for more than 25 years. Her poetry has appeared in a small multitude of magazines, both online and in print. She is the author of numerous poetry chapbooks, recently including a collaboration with j/j hastain called "Dive Back Down" (Dancing Girl Press, 2015), an individual collection called "From One Ruined Human to Another" (Cringe-Worthy Poets Collective, 2018), and with another individual collection, "Another Set of Ripped Out Bloody Pig Tails" forthcoming from The Poet's Haven.

Cook's first full-length individual poetry book, "Horrific Confection", was published by BlazeVOX in late 2008, ten years ago now. Her more recent full-length poetry book, "A Red Witch, Every Which Way, is a collaboration with j/j hastain published by Hysterical Books in 2016. Her MOST recent individual full-length poetry book is this one, "Malformed Confetti".

The poems within "Malformed Confetti" range from 2008 to 2015. In early 2010, Cook suffered from an unexpected Carotid Artery Dissection, which lead to an Aneurysm which lead to a Stroke. Later in 2010, while on the brink of divorce and temporarily living with her parents, Cook began to assemble and submit an earlier version of this manuscript. As time went on, she revised it, added more recent poems, and rearranged it, forming it into a dissected but interconnected discombobulation of pre-stroke and post-stroke work.

Cook's poetic style has undergone changes over the years, but her passion for poetry lives on.

Cook also sometimes creates semi-abstract painting collage art hybrid creatures.

Cook also runs her own tiny independent press, Blood Pudding Press, which sometimes publishes hand-designed poetry chapbooks and sometimes sells art.

## Acknowledgments & Notes

Some of the poems within this collection, sometimes in different versions and/or with different titles, have previously appeared within the following literary publications: Abjective, Action Yes, A Fistful of Razors, Apocryphal Text, Barn Owl Review, Black Heart Magazine, Blasphemy, Blossombones, Caketrain, Certain Circuits, Combatives, Counterexample Poetics, Decomp, Denver Syntax, Diode, Finery, Gargoyle, Hermeneutic Chaos, Horse Less Review, Housefire, Instant Pussy, Listenlight, Menacing Hedge, Nuit Blanche: Poetry for Late Nights, Poets and Artists Self Portrait Issue, Oranges & Sardines, O Sweet Flowery Roses, P.F.S. Post, Plath Profiles, Rain Fade, Scapegoat, Sein und Werden, Skidrow Penthouse, Spider Vein Impasto, Spooky Boyfriend, Strange Girl Press, Taiga, The 6S Review, The Nepotist, Turntable & Blue Light, Lustre, Wicked Alice, and Zero Ducats. Thank you to the editors of these publications.

The poem "Marmalade Glaze" had some of its pieces used within an article called "Storie di non ordinaria femminilità: suzioni, iniezioni, mutazioni" ("Tales of unordinary womanhood: suctions, injections, mutations"), written by Letizia Merello and published on ARTEROTICA in October 2010.

Some of the poems within this collection, sometimes in different versions and/or with different titles, have previously appeared within the poetry chapbooks listed below:

—BONE-BODICED, published by Blood Pudding Press & ISMS Press, 2008 (SOLD OUT) ("Doll Head Obscenity," "Dead Raven," "The Pig Box," "Broken Blister Pearls")

—CARNIVORACIOUS, published by Blood Pudding Press, 2008 (SOLD OUT) ("Snake in a Can Gag")

—PROJECTILE VOMIT, published by Scantily Clad Press, 2008 ("Mass Production," "Plague," "Mutating Cosmetic Surgery")

—MONDO CRAMPO, published by Dusie Kollektiv 3, 2008 ("Cleavage")

—PINK LEOTARD & SHOCK COLLAR, published by Spooky Girlfriend Press, 2009, (SOLD OUT) ("Necking," "Catwalk," "Self-Lubricating," "Purple Speculum")

—TONGUE LIKE A STINGER, published by Wheelhouse Press, 2009 ("Deer Head Variations," "Ghost Teeth," "Parasitic Twin," "A Song," "Sieve," "Hydra," "Another Medusa")

—FONDANT PIG ANGST, published by Slash Pine Press, 2009 ("assembly line doll head roach hotel," "Balut," "Stubble," "Meat Chorus," "Domestic Disturbance," "The New Witchery")

—SOFT FOAM, published by Blood Pudding Press for Dusie Kollektiv 4, 2010 ("Haunted Sea Urchin," "Giant Squid")

—POST-STROKE, published by Blood Pudding Press for Dusie Kollektiv 5, 2011 ("Marmalade Glaze," "Red Shrink Wrap," "Mauvette Maroon," "Angioplasty Show," "Crepuscular Creep")

—POISONOUS BEAUTYSKULL LOLLIPOP, published by Grey Book Press, 2013 ("Say she had dirty follicles," "Ladyfingers," "Venus Tree," "The Ugly Duckling," "The Moth," "The Swan," "The Sugar Glider," "Volatility," "Coiled," "Red Moon Ashes," "Red Lunatic," "Sucker Punch," "Contorted Impregnation," "Spew," "Spawning")

—RED DEMOLITION, published by Shirt Pocket Press, 2014 ("Saint Lucy Eyes," "Love Can Be a Chokecherry," "Why I Dye My Hair Red," "Blue Marriage," "Vintage Pom Pom Underwater," "Insecticide Dye Job," "How Many Holes Can You Handle?")

\*\*\*

The poem "Dead Raven" includes five single lines (1, 5, 9, 13, 17), taken from "The Raven" by Edgar Allen Poe.

The poem "Broken Blister Pearls" was partially inspired by the short film "BOX" by Takashi Miike.

The poem "Fortune Teller" was partially inspired by Gothic Moths, with blackish forewings and a network of fine white lines, supposedly reminiscent of some elements of gothic architecture. These Moths are strongly attracted to sugar and flowers, ranging from Wormwood to Forsythia to Nettle. Some of the poem's text in part two was culled from the Cremaster section on Cocoon.org.

The poem "Blue Marriage" was partially inspired by some poems by Laura Madeline Wiseman, which were partially inspired by tales of Bluebeard.

The poems "Deadly Doll Head Dissection," "Coiled," "dream about being," "Marmalade Glaze," "Red Shrink Wrap," "Mauvette Maroon," "Angioplasty Show," "Crepuscular Creep," "Arterial Discombobulation," "Love Can Be a Chokecherry," "Blue Marriage," "Why I Dye My Hair Red," "Contorted Impregnation," "My sorrow is not something you can eat," "Spew," "Spawning," and "Viral Spiral," were all partially inspired by/related to a health issue the poet suffered from, a Carotid Artery Dissection, which led to an Aneurysm, which led to a Stroke, which resulted in Aphasia and which also seemed to result in her divorce exactly one year later.